Can It Float?

by Bailey Carroll

D0290009

SCHOLASTIC INC.

Photos ©: cover background and throughout: leungchopan/Shutterstock; cover main: Don Arnold/Getty Images; 2: El Choclo/Shutterstock; 3: Incredible Arctic/Shutterstock; 4: Wunson/Shutterstock; 5: Stas Moroz/Shutterstock; 6: David W Hughes/Shutterstock; 7: ViliamM/iStockphoto; 8: Christopher Ray Robertson/Shutterstock.

Designed by Amy Lam.

ISBN-13: 978-0-545-64831-8
ISBN-10: 0-545-64831-9

15 16 17 18 19 20   132   27 26 25 24 23 22 21

Scholastic Inc., 557 Broadway, New York, NY 10012

A leaf can float
on water.

The ice can float
on water.

A boat can float
on water.

The flower can float
on water.

A ball can float
on water.

The swan can float
on water.

Can the frog float on water?